CHARLES EASTMAN

By Betsy Lee

DILLON PRESS, INC.
MINNEAPOLIS, MINNESOTA

Dillon Press, Inc., 500 South Third Street
Minneapolis, Minnesota 55415

Printed in the United States of America

Library of Congress Cataloging in Publication Data

Lee, Betsy, 1949-
    Charles Eastman.
    (The Story of an American Indian ; 27)
    SUMMARY: A biography of Dr. Charles Eastman, doc-
tor, writer, lecturer, and worker for Indian rights, pride, and
a maintenance of and appreciation for their culture.
    1. Eastman, Charles Alexander, 1858-1939—Juvenile lit-
erature.   2. Santee Indians—Biography—Juvenile literature.
3. Physicians—United States—Biography—Juvenile literature.
4. Dakota Indians—Juvenile literature. [1. Eastman, Charles
Alexander, 1858-1939. 2. Santee Indians—Biography. 3. Indians of North America—Biography]   I. Title.
E99.S22E185   970'.004'97 [B] [92]   79-9193
ISBN 0-87518-175-9

CHARLES EASTMAN

A little boy named Ohiyesa was among the Santee Sioux
driven from their Minnesota homeland in 1863. For most
of his boyhood, he thought he was an orphan. When
he was fifteen years old, his father came to the camp in
the Canadian wilderness where the boy was living and
brought him back to the United States. In the years that
followed, Ohiyesa became Dr. Charles Alexander Eastman.
He lived in two worlds—the Indian and the white. He also
lived at a time when native Americans were being forced
to change their way of life. As a young man, he saw
his people lose their freedom. Before he died in 1939, he
saw them bring new life to their culture and their hopes
for the future.

Charles Eastman worked for his people's welfare in
important ways. As a young doctor, he cared for their sick.
Later, as a writer and speaker, he showed the richness
of native American culture to white Americans. He was
the most famous American Indian of his time, and thus
a spokesman for those who could not speak for themselves.

Contents

CHAPTER 1

A New Land,
A New Name

Ohiyesa was five years old when he and his people, the Santee Sioux, were driven from their homeland by Colonel Sibley's army. The soldiers came in great numbers, marching across Minnesota and into Dakota Territory. They chased the Indians north and west to the banks of the Missouri River.

The warriors fought bravely as the women and old men made boats of buffalo hide and branches to carry their children and belongings across the river. Once they reached the other side, the Santee used their horses to get away. The frightened children were strapped in the saddles or held in front of older brothers and sisters. Their horses galloped hard and fast. At night they could not stop to eat or sleep because the soldiers were close behind.

And so Ohiyesa's people were forced to leave their own country and settle in Canada—a country they did not know.

Behind them they had left a land that sparkled with clear lakes and rivers. The Sioux called their homeland Minnesota, which means "land of sky-blue water." They had lived there long before Europeans came, perhaps ten to twelve thousand years ago.

In the 1600s French fur traders heard about a strong

Ohiyesa and his family crossed the Missouri River in little boats like these to get away from the soldiers on their trail.

people who lived in a land of great forests and many streams. The Chippewa Indians living by the Great Lakes called them the "Nadouessioux," which in their language means "snakes." They were old enemies. The French found it hard to say Nadouessioux, so they shortened the name to Sioux.

The Chippewa and Sioux had been bitter enemies for a long time. When the Chippewa were given guns by the European traders, they became stronger than their Sioux rivals. They drove the Sioux from the northwoods to the prairies in southwestern Minnesota.

Some of the Sioux tribes wandered farther west where the buffalo were more plentiful. They gave up their woodland ways and learned to live on the great western plains. By 1800, the Sioux Nation reached from Minnesota to the Rocky Mountains.

The Santee were the "people of the farther end." They guarded the eastern border of Sioux country. It was not easy for them to stay in Minnesota because the Chippewa still fought fiercely with the Santee. With each battle the Chippewa tried to push them a little farther west.

But it was not the Chippewa who finally forced the Santee to leave their homeland. It was the great westward movement of white settlers who pushed into Santee country during the 1800s.

The U.S. government had promised the Indians that no white people could settle in Indian Territory. But the settlers could not be stopped. They crossed into Indian lands by the thousands. Some were bound for California in search of gold. Others stayed to farm the rich land they found in Minnesota.

Over the years, the Indians were persuaded to give up their lands by signing treaties. These agreements promised that the U.S. government would pay for the land that was taken. In 1851 the Santee Sioux gave up their claim to almost all of their homeland by signing two treaties. The treaties left seven thousand Indians only two narrow strips of land along the upper Minnesota River. Each reservation was twenty miles wide and about seventy miles long.

Then the white settlers swarmed into Minnesota in even greater numbers. Settlements grew into towns. Roads were built. Schools, churches, and newspapers were established. And in 1858 Minnesota became a state.

While the white settlements prospered, life on the Santee reservations went from bad to worse. The Indians had been promised payment for their land. It did not come. They were promised food. None came. A crop failure in

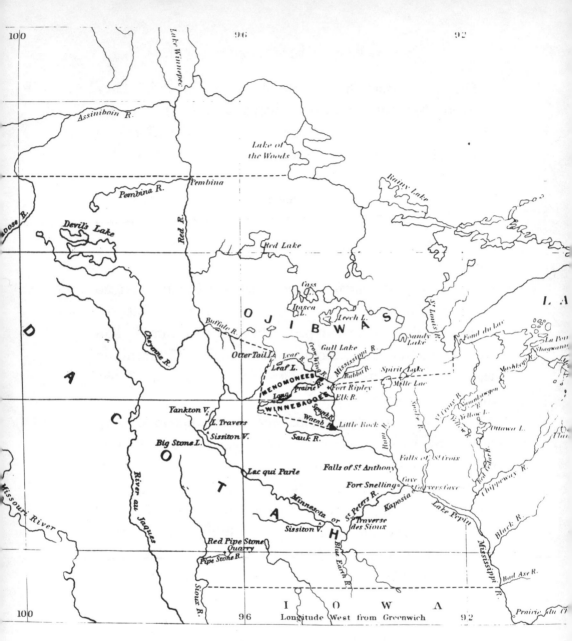

This map, reprinted from History of the Indian Tribes in the United States *by Henry Schoolcraft, shows the boundaries for the Sioux and Chippewa nations as they stood in 1851. "Dacotah" is another name for Sioux, and "Ojibwas" refers to the Chippewa. We have used names which Charles Eastman used for his people and their neighbors.*

1861 caused many of the Santee to die of starvation.

After so many broken promises, the Sioux grew angry and attacked the whites. Led by Chief Little Crow, they swept upon towns and farms, killing the settlers and burning their homes and barns. The uprising ended with the hanging of thirty-eight Sioux warriors at Mankato on December 26, 1862.

Although most of the war chiefs and warriors were dead or in prison, the whites wanted all the Sioux driven out of Minnesota. This gave the settlers a chance to take the rest of their land without payment.

Colonel Sibley, commander of the Minnesota army, led a force of 3,200 soldiers to push the Santee beyond the borders of the state. This was how Ohiyesa found himself bobbing up and down in a buffalo-skin boat on the Missouri River.

Ohiyesa was too young to understand why his family and friends were being chased away from their homeland. To him the journey was just a boyish adventure. Even so, he was sad when he learned that he could never return to Minnesota. Ohiyesa had fond memories of the days when his people had lived there in peace.

The happiest time of his young life had been the day he was given a new name. It was given to him during the mid-summer feast that was held for all the bands of the Santee Sioux. That year, Ohiyesa's band, the Wahpetonwans or "Leaf-Dwellers," had the honor of hosting the feast.

It had been a time of great excitement. Everyone joined in the games and dances. There was plenty to eat and plenty of gift giving.

Towards the evening of the last day of feasting, a medicine man appeared in the circle of the general assembly. This man had made the ball for the lacrosse game that was the high point of the feast. Now he was giving the ball to the warriors, for the game was about to begin.

Beside him stood a little boy. The child's brown body was painted according to custom. His glossy black hair was braided and wound around his head. In each ear he wore a bit of swan's down. He held a tiny bow and arrows.

The little boy was known by the name of Hakadah, which means "the pitiful last." He was the youngest of five children. His mother was very sick after he was born. Before she died, she gave her new baby to her husband's mother to care for as her own. This is why the motherless boy had such a sad name. Today, the warriors of his band would be given a chance to win a new name for him, for this is what the medicine man told the crowd.

"Wahpetonwans, you boast that you run down the elk," he began. "Kaposias, you claim that no one has a lighter foot than you. Either you or the Leaf-Dwellers will have to drop your eyes and bow your head when the game is over. If the Wahpetonwans should win, this little warrior shall bear the name Ohiyesa [winner] through life; but if the Light Lodges should win, let the name be given to any child appointed by them."

After he had spoken, everyone hurried toward the playing field to watch the game. Wagers were made about the outcome of the contest, for the Sioux were great gamblers. Even the most friendly of games was not played without bets.

Lacrosse was invented by the Indians. It was a rough game, and there was no limit to the number of players. The soft ball, made of buckskin stuffed with hair, was tossed from player to player using long sticks with netted pouches. Goal lines were drawn on opposite ends of the playing field. The first team to send the ball over the other's goal would be the winner.

The players had painted their bodies as they did to frighten their enemies in battle. The winning team would be praised as if they had actually won a war. Bets collected after the game were like prize horses taken in a raid. Each man on the winning side would be sure of success in his next raid because the spirits favored him.

A tall, broad-chested warrior strode out into the middle of the field and gave a loud call. At once the little black ball was tossed high above the heads of the players. Cheers and war whoops came from the sidelines. No one shouted louder than Hakadah, who wanted a new name.

Both teams played hard. They pushed one another, and often hit opponents on the head with their long-handled

A game of lacrosse as it was played by the Sioux.

rackets. The crowd watching the game could see only a hundred lacrosse sticks smashing against each other and a mass of painted bodies in a cloud of dust.

The ball flew through the air over the warriors' heads. First one side crept ahead and then the other.

Suddenly, a man broke free from the tangle of players. It was Antelope, the fastest of the Wahpetonwan runners. The Leaf-Dwellers gave a mighty cheer. Antelope threw down his lacrosse stick and clutched the ball in his hand, flying like the wind toward the enemy goal. With one final leap, he won the day for the Leaf-Dwellers.

In the victor's camp there was great rejoicing. Everyone shouted and danced. Drum beats echoed like thunder down the valley. It had been a perfect day. As the setting sun slipped behind the trees, the whippoorwill began its evening song.

All the Santee gathered in a great assembly. Within the circle sat members of the common council, the tribal leaders. Blue Earth, chief of the Leaf-Dwellers, rose to his feet. In memory of this victory, he declared, the boy would now receive his name.

The little boy was led into the circle. All eyes were on him. He stood alone, trembling like a frightened fawn. Chank-yuhah, the medicine man, raised his hand to quiet the cheering. Then he spoke.

"Ohiyesa [winner] shall be thy name henceforth. Be brave, be patient, and thou shalt always win. Thy name is Ohiyesa."

CHAPTER II

Ways of the Wilderness

As Ohiyesa's people wandered north toward Canada, they came upon a wilderness like that they had once known in Minnesota. Great herds of buffalo roamed over rolling yellow plains. The forests were filled with deer and elk and birds of every kind. Here was land that had not been fenced in and plowed by white settlers.

For all his friends and family knew, Ohiyesa was now an orphan. His father had been taken captive after the Sioux Uprising. Everyone thought that he had been hanged along with the other warriors in Minnesota. Ohiyesa was given his boyhood training by his uncle, White Footprint. This man would be a father to him for the next ten years of his life.

It was White Footprint's duty to teach Ohiyesa how to survive in the wilderness. Ohiyesa's uncle was a stern teacher. In the morning when Ohiyesa was sound asleep, White Footprint would give a loud war whoop over the boy's head, or shoot a gun just outside the tipi. Ohiyesa was expected to jump up, grab a weapon, and give a yell in reply. In this way, he was taught to be prepared for an enemy attack at any moment.

These things were not easy for a young boy to learn, but

as Ohiyesa later wrote in his book, *Indian Boyhood,* "I wished to be a brave man as much as a white boy desires to be a great lawyer or even President of the United States."

Ohiyesa was a good rider and an accurate shot with a bow and arrow. White Footprint was among the best hunters of his tribe. Ohiyesa listened carefully to his uncle's teaching because he, too, wanted to become a great hunter.

When Ohiyesa left the tipi in the morning, his uncle would tell him to look closely at everything he saw. When he came back that night, White Footprint would ask him many questions: "On which side of the trees is the light-colored bark? When do you find the fish-eating birds?"

Ohiyesa became a student of nature. Instead of studying books, he studied the habits of animals. He learned to recognize a deer track, to search for the signs of fish in a creek, and to give bird calls.

He and his friends learned to hunt both in the forests and on the plains. While their fathers hunted elk and bear in the fall, the boys were busy shooting chipmunks with their bows and arrows. During the summer buffalo hunt, the boys snared prairie dogs and climbed tall trees to snatch young birds from their nests.

When they weren't hunting, they played games to improve their skills. They practiced with their bows and arrows, raced their ponies, and played "hunting buffalo."

One of their games was waging war against wild bees. Pretending that the bees were enemies, the boys would attack a nest with great courage. The battle was always followed by a make-believe scalp dance.

The first time that Ohiyesa played this game, he went with Little Wound, a very small boy, who was eager to

The summer buffalo hunt required great riding skill and expert marksmanship.

show his bravery. The older boys attacked the nest, knocked it to the ground, and ran away as the bees swarmed after them. But not Little Wound. He jumped on the shattered nest and shouted, "I, the brave Little Wound, today kill the only fierce enemy!"

As soon as he said this, the boy began to scream. One of his friends yelled, "Dive into the water!" Little Wound raced to a nearby lake. When he returned, the other boys did not let him dance with them. They said that he had been killed by their enemy, the Bee tribe. Little Wound watched the dance with a sad, swollen face. He would never forget that he had shown weakness by screaming.

When Ohiyesa wasn't playing with his friends or learning to hunt with his uncle, he spent time with his grandmother. She taught him the beliefs of his tribe. The Sioux believed that a godlike spirit lived in the wild and controlled all things. This spirit they called the "Great Mystery."

When Ohiyesa was eight years old, his grandmother told him that it was time to make his first offering to the Great Mystery. Eager to please her and to receive courage from the Great Mystery, Ohiyesa said, "Grandmother, I will give up any of my possessions!" He would gladly give his bow and arrows, his bear claw necklace—even his pony.

But when his grandmother said that the offering must be Ohiyesa's dog, he could not speak. Tears ran down his cheeks as he thought of losing this friend and companion. And yet he told his dog to be brave as he prepared it for death. He sang a death song for his dog and hugged him tight. Then he walked with his grandmother away from camp to a lonely spot above the Assiniboine River. Ohiyesa gazed at the quiet beauty around him. Surely, he thought, he was in the presence of the Great Mystery. Just thinking about the Great Mystery made his sorrow go away.

After the dog was killed, Ohiyesa's grandmother scattered paints and tobacco around its body as part of the ritual. The boy and his grandmother stood silently for a few moments. Then the old woman began to pray:

"Oh, Great Mystery, we hear thy voice in the rushing water below us! Behold this little boy and bless him. Make him a warrior and a hunter as great as thou didst make his father and grandfather."

Now that Ohiyesa had made his first offering, he was on his way to becoming a warrior.

Even when Ohiyesa was a baby, his grandmother had sung lullabies to him that spoke of great deeds in hunting and in war. From his earliest years, Ohiyesa was urged to

The village where Ohiyesa lived with his grandmother and uncle looked much like this one.

be a champion of his people. One day he would be called upon to defend them with his courage and skill.

Every evening in the Sioux camp, the children huddled around the fires in their tipis and listened to stories of their ancestors. In this way, they learned the legends of their tribe and hoped that one day they might become heroes, too. The young ones were expected to learn these stories by heart and repeat them the next evening. Family and friends would listen carefully as their children spoke and praise them if they told a tale well.

When Ohiyesa was a boy, he enjoyed listening to his uncle's adventures. One evening by the fire, White Footprint told him about the time he had wrestled with a mountain lion and another time when he was almost trampled by a charging buffalo herd.

Ohiyesa watched the fire burning low on that long winter evening. His eyes grew heavy with sleep. He said goodnight to his uncle and his grandmother, who had been listening while she beaded a pair of moccasins.

As he rolled himself up in his buffalo robe, Ohiyesa thought about his uncle's last words: "All this life is fast disappearing, and the world is becoming different."

CHAPTER III

The Spade and
the Pen

One fine morning in September Ohiyesa returned to camp after the daily hunt. He was fifteen years old, nearly a man. Instead of bow and arrows, he carried a rifle, which his uncle had given him on his last birthday. There was an unusual stir in the camp that day. Two strangers wearing white men's clothing had come to the Santee village. Ohiyesa's face burned as his uncle walked toward him with one of these men.

Ohiyesa hated the very sight of white men. They had chased his people from their homeland and had killed his father and older brother. The boy was eager for the day when he could avenge their deaths.

His uncle introduced the man as Many Lightnings, Ohiyesa's father. The boy could not believe it. Had his father not been killed by the white men?

Ohiyesa listened with amazement as his father told him that he was no longer called by his Santee name. He was now an American citizen, and his name was Jacob Eastman.

Then Ohiyesa's father told him how this great change had come about. After Colonel Sibley's army had chased them out of Minnesota, the Santee Sioux scattered in many directions. Families and friends were separated. While

Ohiyesa fled with his uncle and grandmother to the wilds of western Canada, his father and oldest brother had stayed in central Canada.

In the winter of 1863, Many Lightnings and thirty or forty others were caught by U.S. soldiers. They were brought back to Minnesota as prisoners for taking part in the Sioux Uprising. In prison Many Lightnings met Dr. Alfred Riggs, a missionary who talked with him about the Christian faith. Many Lightnings became a Christian and was baptized as Jacob Eastman.

Ohiyesa's father came to accept the whites' way of life as well as their religion. He swore never to take part in an Indian uprising again and to leave the Indian ways of roaming and hunting. Those ways, he knew, were dying out

Ohiyesa's father, Jacob Eastman.

fast. Farms and towns now stood where once there were forests and unbroken plains.

Jacob Eastman spent four years in prison. When he was freed, he went to a Santee reservation, but he was not happy there. He remembered his promise to himself. He wanted to learn a new way of life. He also wanted his children to feel at ease in that way of life.

Under the Homestead Act, a law passed in 1862, a person who was a citizen or was going to become a citizen, could claim 160 acres of public land. All that was needed was to live on the land and farm it for five years. Eastman wanted both land and citizenship.

He laid claim to a plot of land and asked other Sioux families to join him. Together they started a settlement at Flandreau in Dakota Territory and learned how to earn their living by farming. The first years were hard going. Grasshoppers destroyed their crops. Drought caused even more crop failures. It was all that Jacob and his oldest son, John, could do to stay alive. Some people went back to the reservation, but others stayed and began to make a good living. Among them were Jacob and John Eastman.

As soon as he could leave the farm, Jacob set off in search of his other children. Ohiyesa was the only child he found. What happened to Ohiyesa's other brothers after they escaped with their grandmother and uncle, we do not know. It was not an easy life in the wild. They may have died from sickness. They may have been killed in an enemy raid. They may have left the band to marry and begin families of their own.

Now Jacob planned to take his youngest son back to Flandreau. He brought white man's clothes for Ohiyesa. At first the boy refused to wear clothes made by the people he hated so much. On their trip back to the United States, Ohiyesa remembered, "I felt as if I were dead and traveling to the Spirit Land, for now all my old ideas were to give place to new ones, and my life was to be entirely different from that of the past."

Ohiyesa was surprised to find that his father no longer lived in a tipi. Instead, he had built a log cabin on his farm. The boy was baptized like his father and was given a new name. Now he would be known as Charles Alexander Eastman. The name "Eastman" came from Ohiyesa's mother, Nancy Eastman. Her father, Seth Eastman, had been a white man. For the rest of his life, Ohiyesa would use both his Sioux and white names. His Sioux name was still precious to him.

Jacob Eastman was eager for his son to start school. At school Charles would learn the English language and learn to read books. His father called these the "bow and arrows" of the white people.

To Charles, these were strange weapons indeed. When he first went to the little schoolhouse near home, the teacher spoke in a language that he could not understand. Then the teacher drew signs on the blackboard and asked the children to read them. Charles thought the signs on the blackboard were not nearly as interesting as the bird tracks he liked to study in the sand. He longed to return to Canada where his uncle would teach him to hunt and shoot. "They might as well try to make a buffalo build houses like a beaver as to teach me to be a white man," he thought.

After his first day of school, Charles did not want to go back, but he obeyed his father. He went to school every day, even though he did not know what reading books had to do with hunting—or even planting corn.

Charles was not sure of anything anymore. Should he leave the past behind and learn a new way of life? To answer this question, he sought the Great Mystery in the silence of the woods. He spent many hours alone, thinking about what he should do. When he came back, he had made his decision. As a young warrior, he had been taught to dare anything. He would be brave and follow the new trail, even if he did not know where it would end.

In the fall of 1874, he left the Indian settlement and traveled 150 miles to Santee, Nebraska, to go to a boarding school. The school at Santee had been started by Dr. Riggs, the missionary whom Jacob Eastman had met in prison.

Charles crossed the prairie in a homemade wagon with a friend from Flandreau called Peter. The two boys slept in a tipi and shot wild game for their supper. The Big Sioux River Valley was a trapper's paradise, alive with otter, mink, and beaver. Peter changed his mind about going to school. Charles, too, wanted to stay, and yet he had promised his father that he would go to school. It was hard to leave his gun with Peter and start for Santee on foot.

Without a rifle, Charles could no longer hunt for his supper. Along the way he stopped for food at the farms that dotted the prairie. He offered to pay the farmers for his meals, but they let him keep his money. Their friendliness warmed the boy. He became less afraid of white people and wanted to learn more about them.

On the road to Santee, Charles met Dr. Riggs. The missionary spoke the Sioux language very well, and Charles liked him right away. Charles's older brother John, an assistant teacher, met him at the school and introduced him to his new life.

John gave him a suit of clothes and asked someone to cut his hair. "I felt like a wild goose with its wings clipped," Charles remembered.

Charles Eastman in his student days.

At school Charles learned to spell and count. To him, it seemed that white people measured everything in time or money or distance. This was new because Indians did not keep track of anything in their free life. Later, he wrote in one of his books, "We never had had any money to count, nor potatoes, nor turnips, nor bricks. Why we valued nothing except honor: that cannot be purchased!"

At first these things made no sense at all to the boy. But little by little he began to see that the white people's system of counting and writing down what they wanted to remember were their methods of doing business. These things had great importance in their way of life.

Charles studied harder than any of his classmates. By the end of his second year, he had read all the books at the school that were printed in the Sioux language. He had caught up with boys who were several years ahead of him and had begun to study algebra and geometry.

Dr. Riggs knew that Charles was an outstanding student. Since the school offered only a basic education, he arranged for Charles to go to Beloit College in southern Wisconsin. Beloit had a department that prepared students for four-year colleges, much like the high schools of today. This time, Charles was eager to go.

Just as he was leaving for Beloit, he learned that his father had died after a sudden illness. The sad news made him even more determined to obey his father's wishes. Jacob Eastman had risked his life to find his son and had set his feet on a new trail. The boy remembered the last words his father had said to him as he left the farm. "If you should not return, your father will weep proud tears."

As the train sped eastward toward Beloit, Charles watched

the farmhouses on the prairie pass by. Soon they were far behind. Farms became villages, and villages turned to towns. At last the train reached a city.

Charles had never seen a city. He walked in a daze along the crowded streets and stared at the shop windows. Someone directed him to an "eating house," where he sat down, wondering what would happen next. A waitress came and asked what he wanted. Charles was so timid that he nodded his head to everything she said—until he had ordered the whole menu!

At Beloit Charles had to work harder than the others to understand what they learned easily. They had gone to school all their lives. Charles was still struggling to learn the English language. At first he was shy and afraid to speak the strange language out loud. But little by little he overcame his shyness and learned to speak it well.

When summer came, he looked for work on local farms to help pay for his schooling. The president of the college wrote a letter about Charles to help him get a job. With this letter in his hand, Charles walked south of town toward the open country. He arrived, tired and hungry, on a farmer's doorstep. The farmer looked suspiciously at him and asked what tribe he belonged to.

"I am Sioux," Charles answered.

"That settles it," said the farmer. "Get off my farm just as quick as you can!"

The farmer had a cousin who had been killed by Sioux Indians the summer before. He hated Indians as much as Charles had once hated the whites.

As he walked down the road, he wondered if the two races would always be enemies. When he showed his letter

Charles (upper left) with the Dartmouth All Round Athletic Team. He was elected captain of the freshman football team and was a prize-winning long distance runner.

to the next farmer, he was glad to find a warm welcome. Charles worked for that farmer all summer. There were no disagreements between the two of them. This was the ideal that Charles had hoped for—white and Indian living in peace under one religious faith. Like his father before him, he came to believe that there should be no more war between whites and Indians. He also felt that Indians must leave their wild life and learn to farm.

"I renounced finally my bows and arrows for the spade and pen," he later wrote. "I took off my soft moccasins and put on heavy and clumsy, but durable shoes." For the first time he began to think and act like a white man.

He knew that he could not go to school for the rest of his life. In the white world everyone had a job. It was time for him to choose what work he wanted to do. His deepest desire was to use his knowledge to help his people, and so he decided to study medicine.

Having started his education ten years later than most students, however, Charles was far from ready for medical school. After three years at Beloit, he did more pre-college work at Knox and Kimball academies. In 1883, he entered Dartmouth College in New Hampshire. After getting his degree from Dartmouth, he went to medical school at Boston University.

When Charles left the university as a doctor in 1890, he was thirty-two years old. He had gone to school for eighteen long years. During this time, the shy boy from the wilderness had become a learned man, at ease with city life.

Much as he loved the narrow streets and flower gardens of Boston, he was eager to return to the Sioux. Now he could put his schooling to work for his people. He was made government physician at the Pine Ridge Indian Agency in South Dakota. Ohiyesa came back to the Sioux as Dr. Charles Eastman, the first Indian to hold such a high position on a reservation.

CHAPTER IV

Death of a Dream

Dr. Eastman's office at Pine Ridge was not nearly as grand as his title. The room was bare except for a desk and a few hard chairs. Wind whistled through the flimsy walls. Everything was coated with dust, but this did not discourage Charles. He laughed to himself, remembering that he, too, had come from the prairie dust.

The young doctor made the best of what little he had to work with. The next day he hired someone to clean his rooms. Then he found an assistant named George. Together they scrubbed the shelves from top to bottom and filled them with cough syrups and ointments.

Once a month, on issue day, all the Indians on the reservation came to the agency. On this day they received their monthly payments, food, and medical help. When Dr. Eastman opened his office on issue day, he saw a great crowd waiting for him. People had come just to get a look at the "Indian white doctor." Charles later remembered, "I was kept on my feet giving out medicine throughout that day, as if from a lemonade stand at a fair."

His first act as the agency doctor was to close the "hole in the wall" between his office and the room where the Indians lined up for their medicine. The white doctors had pushed pills and potions through the hole to their patients without even examining them.

The new doctor was different. He invited his patients into his office and examined everyone who came to him. The Sioux were most surprised when he talked to them in their own language. No interpreter was needed!

Dr. Eastman wrote down the addresses of his patients and promised to visit them. No doctor had ever done this before. The white doctors had never dared to leave the agency buildings. They were afraid to go freely among the Indian people.

But Charles knew that he had to visit his patients in order to help them. With his own money, he bought a horse, saddle, and saddle bags. Soon he was on the road almost day and night. He never refused to answer a call no matter how far he had to travel. Blizzards did not stop him, and he often rode seventy-five miles in a night. The young doctor was happier than he had ever been before.

One day the chief of the Indian police, Captain Sword, came to visit him. "My friend," said Sword, "the people are very glad that you have come. You have begun well; we Indians are all your friends. But I fear that we are going to have trouble."

Captain Sword told the doctor that a new religion was sweeping across Sioux country. Many believed that the Messiah, the Son of God, was coming to earth again as an Indian. If the Sioux were faithful and did the Dance of the Ghosts, the Messiah would return one day to punish the whites and free the Indians from the reservations. At that time white people would disappear from the earth. Great herds of buffalo and wild horses would come back.

Then the Indian people could return to their old way of life.

As Sword spoke, Charles Eastman listened in silence. He was taken entirely by surprise. Daniel Royer, the Indian agent, joined in the talk. He, too, was scared. He called the new faith "the worst thing that has ever taken hold of the Indian race."

The Ghost Dance: these dancers have fallen into a trance and moved to the center of the circle of dancing believers.

Although Agent Royer saw the Ghost Dance religion as a threat to peace, it was not really warlike. Wovoka, the Paiute Indian who had started the faith, was looked upon as the Messiah. He felt that the Great Spirit was speaking through him. Wovoka said that it was the Great Spirit who would cause the white people to vanish.

"You must not hurt anybody, or do harm to anyone," Wovoka told his followers. "You must not fight. Do right always." If the believers followed these teachings and did the Ghost Dance, the Great Spirit would cause the old earth to pass away and with it, the white people. Those who did the Ghost Dance would be saved, and the Indian dead would come to life again. The Ghost Dancers hoped that this would take place the following spring.

As winter came, more and more people joined the dancing. Children no longer came to school, and work stopped on the Indian farms. The white settlers living nearby became frightened. They demanded that soldiers be called in to protect them. Newspapers predicted an Indian uprising.

Charles Eastman advised Agent Royer to be patient and let the new religion fade away. If troops were called in, said the doctor, war might start from misunderstanding. But the agent did not listen to the doctor's warning. He telegraphed Washington: "The Indians are dancing in the snow and are wild and crazy. We need protection and we need it now."

At dawn on November 20, 1890, Charles was awakened suddenly by his assistant. "Come quick!" George shouted. "The soldiers are here!" Charles rushed to the window. He saw a parade of soldiers marching toward the agency. Behind them rattled a Hotchkiss cannon and a Gatling gun in a cloud of dust. The troops pitched their tents and waited.

The soldiers' camp at Wounded Knee before the battle.

Meanwhile, Charles's life had taken an unexpected turn. He had met Elaine Goodale, the supervisor of Indian schools in the Dakotas and Nebraska. From the very first, they had seemed like old friends. Elaine was only twenty-eight years old, but she had traveled widely throughout the West. During his student days Charles had read her articles about Indian education in eastern newspapers. Like Charles, she had gone to college in Boston. The young doctor and the white teacher found they had much in common. Charles had laid his plans carefully. First he would spend a few years helping his people. Then he would set up a doctor's office in the city. That would be the right time for marriage, he had thought, until he met Elaine.

Together, they helped to decorate the agency for Christmas. The missionaries at Pine Ridge hoped that the holiday would help everyone forget the trouble that seemed to be

Elaine Goodale, who became Charles's wife.

coming. Perhaps Christmas would bring a promise of peace. They filled bags of candy for the children. They practiced Christmas carols. They hung ropes of spicy evergreen in the church and put up a Christmas tree. Christmas Day brought a bright spot of happiness to the agency as Charles and Elaine announced their engagement. It did not bring peace.

News came that Sitting Bull, the most powerful of the Sioux war chiefs, had been killed by Indian police on another reservation. Now Sitting Bull's band were fleeing south to Pine Ridge, in the hope that Red Cloud, the last great Sioux chief, could protect them from the soldiers. They were joined by Big Foot's band from the Cheyenne River Agency. Since these Indians were followers of the Ghost Dance, they were thought to be dangerous. Troops were sent out to stop them at Wounded Knee Creek, eighteen miles away from the Pine Ridge Agency.

The morning of December 29 was bright and sunny. At midmorning, the beauty of the day was broken. Gunfire echoed across the eastern hills, announcing to those at Pine Ridge that a battle had begun. Two hours later a horseman rode toward the agency from the east at full speed. At the same time, a man ran on foot to carry news of the battle to the Ghost Dancers camped close to the agency.

As soon as they heard that Big Foot's band had been wiped out by the troops, the Ghost Dancers fled. "The white teepees disappeared as if by magic," Charles Eastman recalled. A few young warriors fired on the police guarding the agency, but Dr. Eastman was able to calm them.

There was also confusion among the Indians who were not Ghost Dancers. They came to the agency in the fear that the soldiers might attack them by mistake. Everyone knew that fighting could break out again at any moment. Charles tried to persuade Elaine to leave while she could still get away safely. She refused to go as long as she could be of help.

At dusk, the soldiers returned to the agency with their dead and wounded. They were quickly cared for by army doctors. The wounded Sioux lay in open wagons in bitter cold as they waited for shelter. Finally, the church, where the Christmas tree still stood, was turned into a makeshift hospital for them.

Church benches were removed and the bare wooden floor was covered with hay and quilts. The wounded Indians, almost all women and children, were laid side by side in rows. Dr. Eastman worked through the night, trying to save as many as possible. Beside him was Elaine.

The next morning a blizzard swept over the reservation,

covering the ground with snow. On the third day the weather cleared. A search party was sent out for those who had been left behind. Charles Eastman led more than a hundred people to the camp at Wounded Knee. They had wagons to carry back any wounded who might be still alive. Several newspaper reporters and a photographer traveled with them to record the event.

The first body was found three miles from the camp. More and more bodies were found buried in the snow. When the search party reached the camp itself, everyone stared in silence. Among the torn-up tipis and scattered belongings

After the battle at Wounded Knee.

lay the frozen bodies of more than two hundred Sioux men, women, and children.

Nearly all of them had been unarmed when the shooting began. A reckless young Indian fired a shot into the air. At the sound of the shot the troops around the camp started firing from all sides. Some soldiers shot their own comrades who stood opposite them. As the Indians tried to run away, the big cannons opened fire, killing them like buffalo.

Charles Eastman was deeply moved by what he saw. Death songs and wailing filled the battlefield as his companions found their friends and family among the dead. "It took all my nerve to keep my composure in the face of this spectacle," the doctor remembered.

Although they had been lying in the snow for two days and nights, some people were alive. Under a wagon, Dr. Eastman found a blind old woman, unhurt except for frostbite. Beneath a mound of snow he found a crying baby girl warmly wrapped in blankets beside her dead mother.

"All of this," said the young Indian doctor, "was a severe ordeal for one who had so lately put all his faith in the Christian love and lofty ideals of the white man." Charles Eastman's religious beliefs and education had taught him to expect the best from white civilization. The horror at Wounded Knee would haunt him for the rest of his life.

Charles Eastman had seen the end of an era. The Sioux nation would never be the great nation it once was. "A people's dream died there," said Black Elk. No longer could the Sioux dream of returning to their old way of life. Their chiefs were all dead, the tribes scattered. With sorrowful hearts, the people went back to their reservations.

CHAPTER V

Fighting for a
Fair Deal

In March all was quiet on the Pine Ridge Reservation. Elaine left her job and went back to Boston to arrange for the wedding. Charles was asked to speak in Chicago at about the same time. He went with Elaine on the first part of her journey.

In Chicago, Charles was surprised to find out that the newspapers were already predicting another Indian war in the spring. That was impossible, he told reporters. There were only a few thousand Sioux left of fighting age, and half of them were Christians. The reporters also believed that the Sioux were to blame for the Ghost Dance War. That could not even be called a war, Charles said. To him, it was just a religious fad that had been unwisely handled. In some tribes it had died down after a while, but in Sioux country it was forbidden by the whites who had power over the Indians. Forbidding the Ghost Dance had caused bad feelings on both sides.

The Sioux had good reason to wish for an end to white people. Little by little, the land set aside for the Indians was reduced. The land that was left was poor for farming, and they could no longer hunt buffalo for food. Hunting, especially by whites who made their living by selling hides, had destroyed the great herds. Then government shipments of food to the reservations were cut. The Sioux were starving, but the reservation officials would not listen to their pleas. Because the Indians were in misery, they saw the Ghost Dance as their last great hope. That hope had finally ended in violence at Wounded Knee.

When Charles returned to Pine Ridge, he found that it was harder and harder to do his work. He worked for the government, and yet the government did not give him what he needed to do his job. He had no way of getting from place to place unless he provided it. He was not sent the medical equipment he asked for. He had to buy medicines and other supplies with his own money. Now that he was getting married, he could no longer pay for these things himself.

Charles wrote to the commissioner of Indian affairs, the

The Pine Ridge Reservation in 1891.

top official in charge of all the reservations, about his problems. The commissioner was a good friend of Frank Woods, the man with whom Charles had lived in Boston. Knowing someone did what the needs of the Indians could not do. To Charles's surprise, he got a horse and buggy, a hospital, and a trained nurse to help him.

After their marriage on June 18, 1891, the Eastmans worked together. Elaine went with Charles when he visited patients in his horse and buggy. She was always ready with bandages and nourishing food. They made friends among the Sioux and invited them to their home. Many evenings were spent telling Indian legends around their large open fireplace. In the spring of 1892 the Eastmans' first child, Dora, was born.

Their happiness at Pine Ridge did not last long. In June 1892, an agent was sent from Washington to make treaty payments to the Indians. Three people were needed to watch the money being counted out to make sure the payments were honest. Dr. Eastman was asked to be one of them.

From time to time the doctor watched the payment going on while he was in his office. He noticed that the money was not being counted in front of the Indians. Many of them did not understand how much they should receive. When the Indians walked out of the office, the traders were close at hand to get as much of their money as possible.

Several Indians told Dr. Eastman that they did not receive all the money that should have been paid to them. The doctor found out that a schoolteacher and a missionary had counted the money for a few of those who did not know how to count it for themselves. They reported that the amount

Many Sioux were living in great poverty with little hope of a better life. This photo was taken at Mendota, Minnesota, in 1893.

was short from 10 to 15 percent. When the special agent was told of this, he said the Indians were mistaken or had lost the missing money.

The complaints grew louder. An investigation was ordered. Dr. Eastman was asked to sign a paper stating that the payment was honest. He refused because he had not seen the full amount paid to each person. Captain Brown, the agent in charge of Pine Ridge, had also been absent much of the time. Even so, he signed the paper to avoid an investigation. When he tried to get Charles to sign, too, the trouble began.

Charles believed that many people had been cheated of their money, and he said so. After a two-week investigation, an inspector from Washington found that Charles was right.

Ten thousand dollars had been kept unjustly from the Indians.

Captain Brown sent a letter to the commissioner of Indian affairs in which he said that Dr. Eastman had been disloyal. He asked that the "irresponsible" doctor be removed as soon as possible.

A second inspector was sent from Washington to look into the matter. This time, the new inspector found nothing wrong. His report was accepted in Washington, and the first investigation was forgotten.

It was not forgotten on the reservation. Captain Brown still wanted to get rid of the trouble-making doctor. For months he found ways to make the doctor's work difficult. Charles could not get the things that were needed for his patients or for his family. When Elaine wrote to Frank Woods about their problems, he, too, wrote a letter to the commissioner of Indian affairs. In that letter Woods called Charles Eastman the finest man he had ever met. It would be a disgrace, he wrote, if the young doctor were fired "because he could not keep silent when he saw his people wronged and robbed."

Captain Brown continued to fire off letters to the commissioner in which he demanded that Dr. Eastman be let go. Charles decided to go to Washington to plead his own case. He met with the commissioner, some senators, and even the president. Charles had faith in these men who held high office. He expected them to set matters right once they learned of the injustice done to his people. But those he met in Washington were no more fair-minded than the officials at Pine Ridge.

Charles returned to Pine Ridge with a heavy heart. It

was not long before he was asked to leave the reservation. He and Elaine were forced to give up their work and their first home. They were bitterly disappointed. Several of their friends who had sided with Dr. Eastman also lost their jobs.

From his first days at Pine Ridge, Charles Eastman had heard stories about the wrongdoings of reservation officials. He had refused to believe these stories. A great government, he knew, would never permit such things. But now he saw that as long as his people had no education or legal protection, they could not get a fair deal from officials on the reservation or in Washington.

Charles was no longer the hopeful young doctor he once was. Wounded Knee had caused him to question his faith in the white people's goodwill toward the Indians. Now he saw that the reservation system had robbed his people of their control over their own lives. "I longed above all things," said Charles, "to help them to regain their self-respect."

The Sioux had new battles to fight. Charles Eastman would be called again and again to defend his people. His war with officials was only the beginning.

CHAPTER VI

In Good Faith

During his last few weeks at Pine Ridge, Charles had spent most of the one hundred dollars a month he earned on medical supplies. The Eastmans had just enough money left to pay their train fare to Saint Paul, Minnesota.

And so it was that in 1893 Charles returned to Minnesota, the land that he loved as a small boy. He hoped that settling there would bring him happiness again. He opened an office in Saint Paul and waited for patients. This time of waiting, he remembered, was the hardest work he had done.

In his spare time, he began to write down his memories of life in the wilderness. Elaine sent her husband's work to a famous children's magazine called *St. Nicholas*. The stories were published and later became the first chapters of Charles Eastman's first book, *Indian Boyhood*.

This was the beginning of his career as a writer. When Charles saw that he could earn money by writing, he began to write more. His growing fame as a writer began to draw patients to his office. He also became known to other doctors, who elected him secretary-treasurer of the Twin Cities Medical Association.

Just as his practice was getting off to a good start, Charles was called again to serve his people. The Young Men's

The city of Saint Paul offered the promise of success to a doctor just beginning his career.

Christian Association was searching for someone to start YMCAs on the Indian reservations. They told Charles that he was the perfect person for the job.

It was not easy for Charles to give up his medical career when it was going so well. He thought about the offer for several months. At Pine Ridge Charles had found that young Indians had a great need to have faith in religious teachings. This was one reason why they had believed so strongly in the promise of the Ghost Dance. Charles was a Christian. He felt that the teachings of Christ would help his people to regain their faith in themselves. The story of Christ was one of faith in the face of great suffering. Indians had suffered greatly, too.

For this reason the doctor agreed to take up religious work among the Indians. He took the job on the condition that the YMCA would train a young Indian to take his place. After the young man was ready to take over the job, Charles planned to return to his career in Saint Paul.

Charles closed his office in the city and left his patients in the care of other doctors. He began to travel for the International Committee of the YMCA in June 1894. Visiting reservations in North Dakota, Montana, and Canada, he tried to set up YMCA groups wherever he went. He always carried his medical bag on trips in case he was needed as a doctor.

In Montana Charles met a Scottish missionary who had been brought to Christianity by an Indian named Joseph Eastman. As the Scot told his story, Charles realized that Joseph Eastman must be his uncle, White Footprint. His uncle had been a father to him up to the age of fifteen, and Charles had not seen him for more than twenty years.

Charles found his uncle farming in a small village of Christian Indians in Manitoba, Canada. A great feast was held in Charles's honor. All of his old playmates were there to greet him. His uncle was so happy that tears came to his eyes. "The Great Spirit had been kind to let me see my boy again before I died," said the old man.

After the feast, Charles visited the grave of his grandmother. Her spiritual teaching still meant much to him. Beside his grandmother's grave, he said the old, old Indian prayers that she had taught him as a boy. "This was one of the great moments in my life," Charles remembered.

When he returned to the United States, Charles continued to travel for the YMCA. He met with groups of young men from the Sioux, Cheyenne, Cree, Chippewa, and other tribes. In log cabins and little frame chapels, he held Bible studies and told them about the Christian God.

From time to time Charles made speaking trips through the East to raise money for his work among the Indians. While visiting Chicago, New York, and Boston, he was taken by social workers to see how poor people lived in the cities. He was horrified.

As an Indian, Charles had been taught that those who had enough for their needs had a duty to share with the poor. In Indian society extremes of wealth and poverty were not allowed. Every member of the tribe was cared for. "These things troubled me very much," said Charles, "yet I still held before my race the highest, and as yet unattained, ideals of the white man."

In the cities Charles saw people living in places that were as unfit, in their own way, as the Indian reservations.

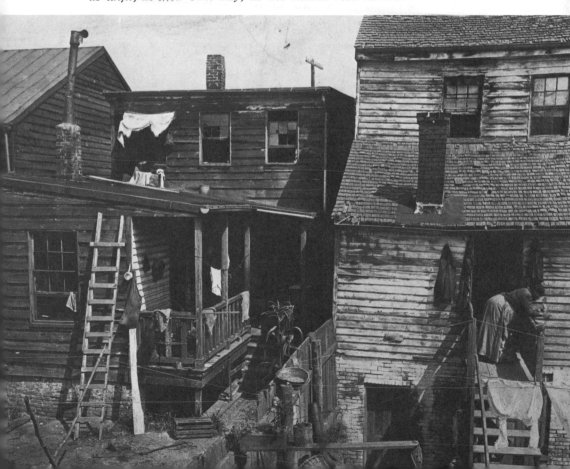

Some of the Indians Charles spoke to became Christians. Many more did not. One old chief of the Sac and Fox tribe rose to his feet to answer Charles after the doctor had talked about his faith.

The old man thanked Charles for coming to visit them. He was glad that Charles was so pleased with the white people's religion and civilization. But his tribe could never accept these. The whites showed neither respect for nature nor reverence toward God. They tried to buy their way into heaven, but they did not even know where heaven was.

"As for us," said he, "we shall still follow the old trail. If you should live long, and some day the Great Spirit shall permit you to visit us again, you will find us still Indians, eating with wooden spoons out of bowls of wood."

A few minutes later, one of the group handed Charles his wallet, which he hadn't noticed was missing. In it were his train tickets and a fairly large sum of money. "Better let these Indians alone!" Charles said to the white missionary beside him. "If I had lost my money in the streets of your Christian city, I should probably have never seen it again."

Charles gave much thought to what had happened. He began to think back to his early religious training. Indian children were taught not to care for money or possessions. They were told to honor nature and the Giver of Life above all else. Their lives were filled with a sense of worship.

Christianity also taught these ideals, but many whites who called themselves Christians did not live by them. "It appears," said Charles, "that they are anxious to pass on their religion to all races of men, but keep very little of it themselves."

Another thing that disturbed him was the way different churches fought to control religious work on the reservations. He saw that this only confused the Indians, who believed in one Great Spirit.

Charles found his YMCA work frustrating. In two years, he had organized only eight new YMCA groups. The YMCA Committee did not seem very interested in paying for its work among the Indians. Charles had to spend a great deal of his time giving talks to raise the funds he needed for the work. After three years, the Sioux Indian whom Charles had chosen to take over his work had gone through the needed schooling. Charles was then able to give up his position with the YMCA.

Charles Eastman had tried to tell his people that the whites' religion was not to be blamed for the evils of their civilization. His faith in the Christ ideal was still strong, but like his people, he was disappointed that the whites did not practice what they preached. "I do not know how much good I accomplished," said Charles of his YMCA work, "but I did my best."

CHAPTER VII

Century
of Dishonor

Charles never went back to being a doctor in Saint Paul. The Eastmans now had three children, and Charles could not afford to set up an office. Once again he was ready to try something new, and once again the Santee Sioux needed his help. The Santee had lost millions of dollars through broken treaties with the U.S. government. The tribal leaders asked Charles to represent them in Washington, D.C.

Charles Eastman was thirty-nine years old when he started his new career. He was not a lawyer, but he was given the power to act in the Indians' behalf. During the next three years, he would defend the rights of his people before the Indian bureau, the Congress, and the president.

Charles went to Washington in 1897 with his brother, John. They began to study the treaties that had been made between the Santee and the United States. The Indians had entered into them in good faith, trusting the government to keep its word. Nearly all of the treaties, the Eastman brothers learned, had been broken. Their task was to get the treaty money that was unpaid after the Sioux Uprising of 1862. "I was confident," said Charles, "that a fair deal would be granted, and our wrongs corrected without undue delay." In spite of what had happened at Pine Ridge, Charles hoped that the national leaders would deal fairly with his people.

The Eastman brothers were treated kindly when they presented their claim in Washington. Charles and John were told that their case would be heard without delay. But as soon as their backs were turned, the Eastmans were ignored.

Before Congress voted on the claims, they had to be brought before certain committees. Charles argued his case before both the House and Senate committees on Indian affairs. He was very discouraged by these meetings. Instead of asking questions about the Indians' claims, the congressmen asked Charles, "Where did you go to school? Why are there not more Indians like you?"

Charles went from one congressman to another, trying to gain support for his cause. He was followed by a swarm of hangers-on, who claimed that they could sway this or that congressman to vote for the claims. Of course, they wanted payment for their influence. Even some of the congressmen wanted to be paid for their votes.

Sometimes Charles carried his case to the president. Over the years, Charles met with four presidents: Benjamin Harrison, Grover Cleveland, William McKinley, and Theodore Roosevelt. Charles and Elaine had entertained Roosevelt in their home at Pine Ridge. Roosevelt was well-liked by the Indians. A Sioux chief said of him: "While he talked, I forgot that he was a white man."

During Roosevelt's second term in office, he, too, disappointed the Indians. They had hoped that their claims would be repaid. "But things seemed to be worse than ever," remembered Charles.

In spite of the Eastmans' efforts, the Indians did not receive any of their treaty money. Charles had not been paid for his work because his payment was supposed to come out of that money. John paid some of his brother's expenses, but by the summer of 1899 Charles was in debt.

He was forced to let John carry on alone. Charles worked first at an Indian school in Pennsylvania, where Elaine had found work. Then the Eastmans moved to South Dakota. For three years Charles was a doctor again at the Crow Creek reservation there.

In the spring of 1903, Charles Eastman was given a new job by the Bureau of Indian Affairs. The bureau asked him to organize all the Sioux Indians into family groups and to give names to each family. The Indians had never needed family names because they knew the history of one another's family. Every person in their band was a relative, and their property was shared by everyone.

In 1887 Congress had passed a law by which every Indian family owned their own land. But without a family name it was difficult to pass on property from parent to child. Even more confusion was caused by the fact that names like "Young Man of Whose Horses the Enemy is Afraid" were not easy to put into English.

There were thirty thousand Sioux living on reservations when Charles Eastman began the renaming project. He wanted to be very careful to keep the meanings of Indian names, which were very important to the Sioux. At the same time the new names had to be short and easily said by white people. Charles first chose a name from the names of the people in the family. All the brothers, their wives, and children were then given this name as a last name.

The Indians wondered why their names were being changed. Charles told them that the project was for their good. It would be easier for them to keep land in their families. But a history of unfair dealings with the whites caused the Indians to doubt him. They said among themselves that this was another trick to steal what little land they had left.

"The older men," said Dr. Eastman, "would sit in my office and watch my work day after day, before being convinced that the undertaking was really intended for their benefit."

Charles's work went slower than he had expected. It was not easy to trace family ties among the Indians. Some Indian children had lost their parents and were adopted by other relatives as Charles himself had been as a child. Just who their parents had been was not always clear. Some of the older men with several wives refused to give their name only to one wife as the law required.

Charles spent six years going from reservation to reservation renaming the Sioux. By studying the family trees of the Indians, he learned a great deal about the history of his people.

As his knowledge of his people grew, Charles gained a new respect for their past. He knew that Indian culture was fast disappearing as the Sioux were forced to take on the white people's ways. All the beliefs and customs of his people might someday be forgotten.

There was a wealth of culture and spiritual depth to Indian life which Charles felt should be saved for the sake of white people as well as Indians. He turned to writing to describe his people's "life from the inside." His first

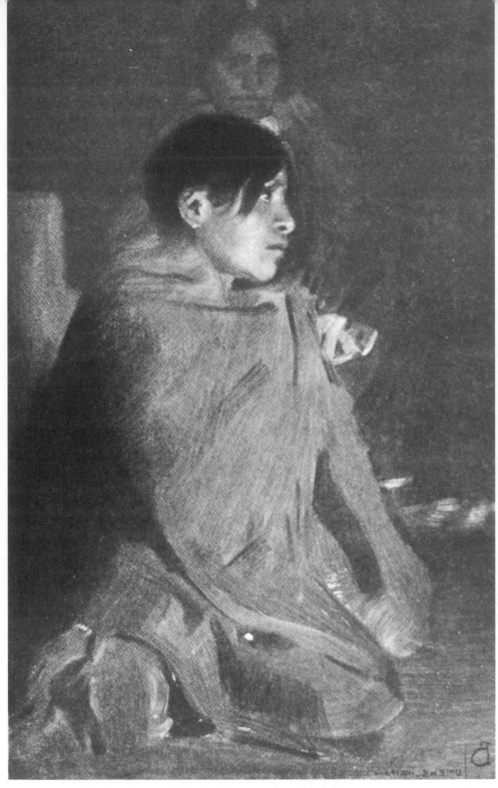

A painting of Charles Eastman as the child Ohiyesa in Indian Boyhood.

book, *Indian Boyhood,* was published in 1902. It was followed by *Red Hunters and the Animal People,* a collection Sioux folk tales, published in 1905. He also wrote many stories for popular magazines that told about the American Indian. During the next few years, Charles Eastman became well known as a writer and speaker. He gave talks in Philadelphia, Baltimore, and Chicago.

On December 31, 1909, Charles left his job with the Indian bureau to spend all his time on writing and lecturing. This, he decided, was the best way he could help his people now.

A century of dishonor had cheated the Indians of their land. Charles had tried to restore these broken treaties, but he failed. The Indians no longer trusted the whites, and the whites did not understand the Indians. Someone needed to interpret the ways of one to the other. Because he had lived in both worlds, Charles Eastman could do this.

"I was a pioneer in this new line of defense of the native American," wrote Charles, "not so much of his rights in the land as his character and religion."

CHAPTER VIII

Spokesman for a Silent Nation

During the next twenty years of his life, Charles Alexander Eastman became the best-known American Indian in the world. He wrote nine books and dozens of magazine stories on Indian life. His books were printed in other languages and read by many outside the United States.

Charles Eastman was also a famous speaker. Dressed in his buckskin costume and headdress, he talked about Indians to schools and clubs. "None of my earlier friends who knew me would have believed that I was destined to appear in the role of a public speaker," said Charles, surprised by his own success.

On his lecture tours Charles traveled widely throughout the United States. Wherever he went, he told the story of the Indians—their inner life, their dreams, and ideals. The deep meaning of Indian ceremonies and customs had never been explained to white people before.

Because Indian culture was different from theirs, they did not understand it. White people had been told that the Indians were devil-worshippers. This was not true, said Charles Eastman. From childhood, Indian boys and girls were given religious training. They were taught to have a deep love for God. Indians did not go to church because

Charles Eastman in the clothing of his people.

they worshipped God in nature. Indian children learned to respect all living things. They had a high standard of honor and friendship. They were taught that a true Indian shares whatever he or she owns.

The people who heard Charles speak were amazed. They

began to look at the American Indian in a new way. All the books and newspaper stories about Indians had been written by white authors who did not understand Indian ways. Charles Eastman told the Indian's side of the story for the first time.

But a tragic thing happened. Even as Charles spoke, the Indians themselves were losing pride in their own culture. Indian children were sent away to boarding schools. They were told never to speak their tribal languages and to forget the traditions of their parents. The old people who stayed on the reservations were not allowed to hold their religious ceremonies. Charles Eastman knew that these ceremonies were a central part of Indian life. The beliefs of the Indians had been passed down for hundreds of years. If they died with the old people now, they would be lost forever.

It was not enough to tell white people about the high ideals of Indian culture. Charles had to restore his people's pride in their own traditions. To do this he helped form social clubs for young Indians who had left the reservations to live in cities. Through these clubs Indians could keep their own beliefs while living in white society. Charles also started a group for young white people who studied the traditions, customs, and outdoor life of American Indians.

Charles Eastman was one of the earliest supporters of the scouting movement. He helped to set up scouting clubs in Boston, New York City, Pittsburgh, and other cities. During the summer of 1914, he was in charge of the largest Boy Scout camp in America. Later that year he wrote a guide for Boy Scouts and Campfire Girls called *Indian Scout Talks*.

In 1915, the Eastman family opened a children's camp

of their own. It was located on Granite Lake in the hills of New Hampshire.

Everyone in the family worked at the camp. Elaine and the three oldest daughters were teachers and counselors. The two younger girls and Ohiyesa, the Eastman's only son, helped with the chores. Charles played games with the children, led hikes through the woods, and taught archery and swimming. The young campers slept in tents, and at night they sat around a huge fireplace, listening to Charles's Indian stories.

The camp was a great success. Then, two years after it opened, tragedy struck the Eastman family. In 1917, a flu epidemic swept the New Hampshire countryside. Irene, Charles's favorite daughter, became ill and died. After her death, the camp at Granite Lake was a lonely place for Charles.

In the years that followed, Charles often came to the camp in fall and spring to be alone and hunt in the woods. But these times of rest were brief. He was needed as a spokesman for his people.

In 1918, Charles was president of the Society of American Indians. This group was the first national organization of Indian leaders. During his year in office, Charles went from town to town speaking to groups of Indians and whites. While Charles was away on his speaking tour during the summer of 1919, Elaine ran the camp at Granite Lake. Not many children came that year, and by 1920, the camp was in financial trouble.

For years now, Elaine had raised and educated their six children by herself. Charles's public life was robbing him of a private life with his family. His many long absences and the lack of money strained his marriage to the breaking point. In August 1921, it ended in separation. Charles gave the camp property to Elaine. Then he went to live with his son Ohiyesa, who was now an advertising executive in Detroit.

Elaine tried to keep the camp open, but fewer children came each year. Finally, in 1924, she was forced to sell the camp at Granite Lake.

These were sad years for Charles. He missed the camp and his family. His children were grown and gone. He had wanted them to share his love for Indian culture, but they had been raised in modern society, far from the wild life Charles had known as a boy.

Charles began working again for the treaty money that the government still owed the Santee Sioux. The Santees' claim was finally settled in the U.S. Court of Claims. Charles received a small fee for his work.

Charles spent the next few years traveling and lecturing. In 1928, he went to England on a lecture tour. He was an honored guest at Oxford and Cambridge universities. Lords and ladies entertained him at their country homes. When they invited him to go fox-hunting, Charles amazed them with his horsemanship. The young Indian boy who once rode bareback over the Dakota plains now looked like an English gentleman in his red riding jacket and top hat.

After a busy two months abroad, Charles returned home to America. He was now seventy years old, one of the most respected Indian leaders of his time. Charles had served his people as a doctor, lawyer, educator, historian, writer, and public speaker. "I was trained to be a warrior and a hunter, and not to care for money or possessions, but to be in the broadest sense a public servant," he wrote in the story of his later life, *From Deep Woods to Civilization.*

In that book Charles Eastman told how his father put his feet on a new trail. As a frightened boy, he had begun his long journey from the deep woods to civilization. It had not been an easy path. Charles had taken on Christianity and the white American way of life. And yet through the years he had lost his faith in their power to bring change for good to his people. Weary of his long struggle, he returned to the deep woods of his boyhood.

With the help of his son, Ohiyesa, he found the perfect spot for a cabin. It lay between Lake Superior and Lake Huron on Wilson Channel. No one else lived on that stretch of shoreline.

Here Charles could enjoy the rest he deserved. He built his cabin forty feet above the water. It could be reached only by stairs and a steep path. The one-room cabin was furnished with a bed, a couple of chairs, oil lamps, and a wind-up phonograph.

From across the channel, his neighbors watched Charles climb down to the shore early in the morning. He would bellow a moose call that echoed across the water. Then he dove into the channel for his morning dip.

Ohiyesa spent his vacations at the cabin with his father. Like Charles, he enjoyed being alone in the wilderness. Ohiyesa had never been close to his father. During the last years of Charles's life, father and son came to know each other for the first time. As Charles grew older, his health began to fail. Ohiyesa made his father promise to give up his moose call and morning dip.

More and more, Charles retreated into memories of the

past. The walls of his cabin were covered with portraits of famous Indians. He had written about their lives and battles in his last book, *Indian Heroes and Great Chieftains*. He loved to point to the pictures and tell stories about each one to his friends. "They were fine men," Charles would say, "but there are no real Indians left."

Charles's neighbors recalled one of the last times they saw the Indian author. Wrapped in a red blanket, Charles stood in a canoe on the channel, watching the evening sun wane westward.

Charles Eastman lived during a time of terrible change for his people. He had seen the Sioux all but destroyed by the coming of the whites. After the fighting finally ended at Wounded Knee in 1890, the Sioux felt they could never return to their old way of life. They were strangers in their own land, surrounded and controlled by those who hoped to stamp out their customs, language, and religion.

But Charles also lived to see a new Indian policy in the 1930s. In 1934, Congress passed a law which restored tribal lands to the Indians and encouraged tribal councils to govern themselves. The new law also granted Indians religious freedom. They could perform their sacred ceremonies openly now.

Charles's message was finally heard. At long last his people would have a voice of their own. Charles Eastman, perhaps more than anyone else, kept Sioux culture and tradition alive during the silent years from 1890 to 1934. Much of what we know today about the American Indian we owe to him.

Charles Alexander Eastman died of bronchial pneumonia on January 6, 1939, at the age of eighty-one.

THE AUTHOR

Betsy Lee is a free-lance writer and
photographer whose illustrated articles
have appeared in the *New York Times,*
the *St. Louis Post-Dispatch,* and several
magazines. While at Chapman College, she
went around the world three times on
Chapman's World Campus Afloat, a
shipboard university. *No Man to Himself,*
a book of poems and photographs taken
in thirty countries, was published as a
result of her travels. Ms. Lee received a
B.A. in English literature from the University of Wyoming. She spent five years in
England and now lives in Minneapolis
with her husband.

*Photographs reproduced through the courtesy of the Dartmouth Col-
lege Library, the International Museum of Photography at George
Eastman House, the Minneapolis Public Library, the Minnesota
Historical Society, the Smithsonian Institution, Anthropological Ar-
chives, the South Dakota Department of Cultural Affairs, and the
South Dakota State Historical Society.*

OTHER BIOGRAPHIES
IN THIS SERIES ARE

William Beltz
Robert Bennett
Black Hawk
Crazy Horse
Geronimo
Oscar Howe
Pauline Johnson
Chief Joseph
Little Turtle
Maria Martinez
George Morrison
Daisy Hooee Nampeyo
Michael Naranjo
Osceola
Powhatan
Red Cloud
Will Rogers
John Ross
Sacagawea
Sealth
Sequoyah
Sitting Bull
Maria Tallchief
Tecumseh
Jim Thorpe
Tomo-chi-chi
Pablita Velarde
William Warren
Annie Wauneka